Published in the United States by Viva Editions, an imprint of Start Midnight, LLC, 221 River Street, Ninth Floor, Hoboken, New Jersey 07030.

Printed in the United States
Cover design: Jennifer Do
Cover image: Shutterstock
Text design: Frank Wiedemann

First Edition.
10 9 8 7 6 5 4 3 2 1

Trade paper ISBN: 978-1-63228-083-1
E-book ISBN: 978-1-63228-140-1

SHUT UP,
YOUR KID IS NOT THAT GREAT

JASON COLE
INTRODUCTION WITH TOM BRADY SR.

V!va
EDITIONS

TABLE OF CONTENTS

A VERY BRADY INTRODUCTION

Tom Brady needed help when he was in middle school and his dad knew it.

Brady's parochial school basketball team featured him, one other good player, and a bunch of guys who, well, weren't very good. Tom Brady Sr. could see the predicament his talented son was in. As volunteer athletic director of the school, Brady Sr. had to come up with an answer to improve the squad.

The elder Brady and his wife had done stuff like this for years. The couple were devoted parents, having raised their three older girls to be great athletes as well. Brady Sr. often coached, and the family built their lives around a sports schedule. There was one year where mom and dad attended and/or coached 314 games.

Brady Sr. would get to work at his insurance agency by 6:00 a.m. so he could make afternoon practice. If you were looking for parents who had their kids' best interests at heart, look no further than the Bradys. Of course, being devout was in the elder Brady's makeup. Before deciding to get married and start a family, he had attended seminary with the idea of becoming a Catholic priest.

At the moment, however, he needed to do something about young Tom's issue on the basketball team in the competitive league of Catholic schools that dot the San Francisco Peninsula.

He came up with a rule. It didn't involve recruiting better players or transferring his son to a new school the way so many other parents would do.

Rather, every kid had to play at least a certain amount of time no matter how good or bad they were.

Yep, all those guys who were challenged to walk and dribble needed to play more, not less.

"A lot of those kids had never played or had a chance to throw or catch a ball. They weren't going to get any better sitting on the bench and not learning. You had to give them a chance," Brady Sr. said.

At a time when parents are increasingly invested—both in terms of time and financial commitment—in getting their children to the best and brightest programs in whatever activity they perform, it's wise to think about how the father of the greatest quarterback in National Football League history didn't put his kid's success ahead of other kids'.

"I was always really conscious of that," Brady Sr. said. "If I put one of my girls at catcher or pitcher or shortstop, I always made sure to double check with my other coach to ask, 'Is she really the best one to play there?'"

It is little wonder that Brady himself is best known among his teammates for sharing credit. When the Tampa Bay Buccaneers held a ring party after winning the Super Bowl in the 2020 season, Brady made a long speech in which he named every player on the team and how they had contributed to the championship season.

As much as everyone in the sporting world knew that Brady was the reason the Buccaneers went from an also-ran in 2019 to a champion the following season, Brady himself was the first to share the spotlight.

That sentiment is at the heart of this book. Yeah, this book is designed to be humorous, and sometimes bitingly so. Welcome to my writing style. But at the core is a pretty basic message: If you want your kid to be a great performer, whether that's in sports or entertainment, you better think about the other people around your kid who are going to help him or her on their journey to greatness.

No matter how good you think your kid is or what other people tell you, shut up about promoting your kid at the expense of those around them. If you want your kid to be surrounded by a great team in sports or a great band in music, make sure he or she knows how to be part of one.

And with that in mind, we're off.

SHUT UP,
YOUR KID IS NOT THE NEXT JOHN ELWAY

Dan Henson took the concept of being an overbearing, helicopter parent to a new level.

He was the "Overpass Dad."

In the late 1990s, Henson's son Drew was going to be the next big thing in sports. Drew Henson was a three-sport star at Brighton High School in Brighton, Michigan. He was the top quarterback recruit in college football and was being wooed by every school in the country. He was drafted in the third round in June 1998 by the New York Yankees. He would have been drafted higher if not for the football part of the equation, although the Yankees were a team that made a habit of taking a chance on two-sport studs such as John Elway, the Hall of Fame quarterback and eventual No. 1 overall NFL Draft pick who dabbled with the Yankees for a year in college.

Anyway, Drew Henson was tagged by many as the second coming of Elway and on August 3, 1998—before Henson had ever set foot on the University of Michigan campus as a student—Henson was featured in an article in *Sports Illustrated*.

That particular day was also the twenty-first birthday of the starting quarterback for Michigan at the time. He was a far-less heralded junior from Northern California who had worked his way up from the number six spot on the depth chart when he arrived in Ann Arbor. To fans at Michigan, it seemed like just a matter of time before Henson leapfrogged the other guy for the job and continued on his path to lead Michigan to glory and become one of the all-time greats in football history.

That Tom Brady guy didn't stand a chance.

In fact, Dan Henson thought his son should have been ahead of Brady from Day 1. On many an occasion, the elder Henson would tell people how difficult it was for his son to split time with the elder Brady in practice.

"This is really hard on Drew," Henson would say, according to members of the team's staff.

And the fact is that Drew Henson was both talented and a good guy in the eyes of most people.

"I really think to this day that if Drew had focused on just football, he would have been a great quarterback," Tom Brady Sr. said. "Splitting time between the two sports just didn't work for him."

If Dan Henson hadn't tried to manipulate things so much, the situation might have turned out differently. Numerous people who encountered the elder Henson tell stories of how Dan would work the system to benefit his son, even when his son didn't need the help. To leverage playing time for his son as a freshman at Michigan, Henson had his son verbally commit to Florida State during the recruiting process. Henson, who had been an assistant football coach at the college level before his son went to Michigan, even became an agent at one point.

But there was more. Dan would show up at Michigan practices. Not just once in a while or even semiregularly. Every day, day after day. The situation quickly became a distraction. Michigan coach Lloyd Carr politely tried to tell the elder Henson not to come by. When Dan Henson kept making appearances, Carr had to eventually put his foot down and tell old man Henson that he couldn't be at practice.

This was in the days when Michigan still practiced outside all the time. Glick Field House had yet to be built. So, Dan Henson came up with another idea on how to watch his son.

Stadium Boulevard on the Michigan campus features an overpass. At the time, the overpass ran right next to the football practice field. Dan Henson would park his car on the overpass, get out, and watch practice.

He was literally the "Overpass Dad."

The whole thing became a running gag within the Michigan football program. To this day, people who saw it just shake their heads and chuckle in disbelief.

"I remember the first time Dan was up there on the overpass," said a member of the football staff. "A bunch of the players just looked up and they were stunned. Then they started laughing. Then we realized how much Drew hated it because his dad just couldn't let go."

While Drew Henson eventually became one of very few athletes with the ability to play in both the NFL and Major League Baseball, his career was only a glimmer of what people expected. He finished his two careers with exactly one touchdown pass in the NFL and one hit in baseball.

SHUT UP,
YOUR MUSICAL TASTE IS OUT OF DATE

The concept of the "Momager" is widely understood in the music, sports, and entertainment world. The "Momager" is the mom (and sometimes dad, although "Dadager" just doesn't have the same ring) who can't let go of her child's career.

In the case of one such mom, the only way her son was going to make it was if the producer went behind her back. The specific singer will go unnamed because the music executive wanted it to remain anonymous, but this male singer had been doted upon so thoroughly by his mother that he was completely incapable of making his own decisions.

"Or if he did make a decision, it was almost always the wrong one," the executive said. This mostly had to do with artistic choices, as the young man traversed the rhythm and blues genre of the early 2000s. As the producers tried to harness his immense talent, they tried time after time to get him to try modern ideas on how to perform.

He and his mother resisted, and his mother fell back on what she liked, which was almost always some sound made big in the 1970s by the likes of Frankie Beverly or Anita Baker.

He was young, good-looking, and hip . . . except when he started to perform. It was like listening to an oldies session. His Momager would smile and dance during the recording sessions as the producers tried time and again to convince the young singer to go in a new direction. Eventually, there was a breakthrough and the producers won a battle against Momager and son, getting him to agree to record a song with modern touches.

The producers and the recording company loved the song. They believed it would be a hit and wanted to build the next CD release around the song. They started talking about how to preview the song, which talk shows they would use to introduce it, and how to use it in concerts.

There was just one problem: Mom and son hated the song. Intensely hated it. They even started arguing about whether to release it at all. The producers had to find a way around them.

So, the producers leaked the song against the wishes of the son and mother. It wasn't a pretty discussion when it got out, but the producers were able to put off the confrontation long enough for the song to become a hit.

"It was his biggest song, and he and his mom hated it," the executive said with a chuckle. "But when the money rolled in . . ."

SHUT UP,

YOUR KID IS NOT THE NEXT GREAT EVANGELIST

Okay, you're from a family of devout faith and you're very generous when it comes to passing around the donation plate. Your kid is also great at encouraging other people to donate to the church and does a really good job of reciting Bible verses.

Maybe he or she even throws in a "Praise the Lord" or "Hallelujah" at the right moments in the sermon.

That doesn't make them the next Joel Osteen.

SHUT UP,
YOUR KID IS A LONG WAY FROM THE BIG SCREEN

Okay, your kid is great at social media, has grown a TikTok following, is pretty creative in the short videos that they post on all the new sites that pop up around the internet, and is damn good-looking. With the right acting lessons, he or she could be a big star. At least that's what you're telling every friend you have who will listen.

Before you get too eager, just pinch yourself and say to yourself, "My kid is not the next Tom Cruise or Jennifer Lawrence."

WAIT A SECOND,
THAT GUY MAKES HOW MUCH FOR DOING THAT?

Most kids love Drake, but face it, your kid is not going to make his professional gaming team of 100 Thieves.

Your kid is not the next Ninja or PewDiePie. But there's no doubt in my mind your kid can make it to level 11 of Super Mario Brothers if they really put their mind to it. Tell your kids there are better things in life to do than watch some random dude playing video games.

SHUT UP,
AND DON'T DRIVE YOUR SON TO WORK

NFL cornerback Eli Apple has had a good enough career that he has lasted seven years in the NFL as of the writing of this book. It just hasn't been the career that either Apple or the New York Giants had hoped it would be when he was drafted with the No. 10 overall pick in the 2016 draft.

"We did a lot of background work on him, and everything seemed to be normal," said a former Giants personnel executive. "We just didn't account for the mom."

Annie Apple, who was a New Jersey native and felt a certain closeness to the Giants as a result, became a star almost as soon as her son was drafted because of her straightforward style with the media. In particular, she loved Twitter and social media, generally. Where things got out of control was how protective she was of her son.

Or perhaps protective of her own status as a football mom. One of the first videos she posted was of her driving Eli to his first day of work with the Giants. While it seemed relatively harmless to most, it didn't go over well with his teammates. Specifically, other players thought Eli was soft and tested him right away.

Worse, first-year head coach Ben McAdoo had little clue how to guide Eli or deal with the perception that the team's first-round pick was immature.

"McAdoo didn't know how to talk to the kid, he didn't know how to talk to the mom, and didn't know how to get the locker room under control," the former executive said. "The two guys under the biggest microscope didn't have a clue how to deal with the pressure. Everybody was trying to help Eli man up, but then his mom was claiming that we were putting pressure on him. We're trying to get him ready to play in the NFL and she's trying to keep the training wheels on him. Total nightmare."

In the end, Eli was cut after three unsuccessful seasons with the Giants and never achieved the kind of acclaim expected of him as such a high draft pick.

SHUT UP,
AND LET YOUR KID GET INTO COLLEGE ON THEIR OWN

I t should surprise exactly no one that the controversy surrounding parents Lori Loughlin and Mossimo Giannulli faking the resumes of their children Olivia Jade and Isabella in an effort to get them into the University of Southern California is hardly something new among wealthy and overbearing parents.

The late Fred Hargadon, who was the Dean of Admissions at both Stanford and Princeton, used to regale associates with absurd stories, ranging from the time an applicant pretended to be the principal of a school to the more serious effort by one father. In the late 1970s, the father in question met Hargadon at a party and offered him $100,000 to admit his child to Stanford, a school with notoriously difficult admissions standards.

Hargadon politely said no . . . on two levels.

"I turned down the bribe and then I really had to make a tough call because the student was actually pretty close to getting in," Hargadon said. "I don't think she would have gotten in, but I remember looking at the application and just shaking my head. The dad killed her chances."

SHUT UP,
YOUR KID'S NOT GOING TO BE
THE NEXT PRESIDENT

While it's many kids' dream to be the president of the United States when they get older, there have only been forty-six presidents, and your kid won't be the fiftieth. If they try really hard, they might be the next class president—if they even still have those at your kid's school.

If not, when they get older, they can always watch reruns of *The West Wing*.

SHUT UP,
YOUR KID'S PERSONALITY ISN'T THAT BIG

Your kid is ruggedly handsome, has the athletic talent to play football in college, and maybe even can hit it big in some "sport" like wrestling because of his combination of flair and humorous facial expressions. Beyond sports, he might even have some acting chops in his future. It's a fabulous combination.

But stop talking about how your kid is going to be the next The Rock. Dwayne Johnson has that gig locked down.

PUTTING A GOLF CLUB
IN YOUR KID'S HANDS AT AGE TWO
GUARANTEES NOTHING

All right, you're thinking way ahead of the curve in this whole sports idea, sort of like a certain parent of a one-time prodigy. Like you, that father put a golf club in his son's hands at two years old and taught his boy to swing hard.

It all came together very naturally with a great swing that took him on to Stanford University and then one of the greatest careers in the history of the game. However, no matter how good your kid becomes by the age of five, don't pretend that he's about to become the next Tiger Woods. You're not Earl Woods, either.

And even Tiger Woods didn't hit a three-iron as well as Elin Nordegren.

BEING A BEST-SELLING AUTHOR
IS NOT QUITE THAT EASY

Just because your child wins a seventh-grade essay contest doesn't mean they're the next Stephen King. Every week there's a limited number of people who make the *New York Times* Bestseller list. Most likely, your kid won't be one of them.

But your child could easily become a writer. Get their byline in the school paper first.

SHUT UP,
WINNING A SHOOTING CONTEST IS NOT ENOUGH

Okay, your kid just won a free-throw shooting contest at school and the local AAU basketball coach is recruiting him for the travel team.

Even if he's really good, there's only a couple hundred players in the NBA. Your kid is five-foot-six, and he won't be the next Spud Webb. So let's just hope he makes the junior varsity basketball team.

SHUT UP,

YOUR DAUGHTER IS NOT
THE NEXT JULIA ROBERTS OR DOLLY PARTON

There was nothing quite so visceral as the show *Toddlers & Tiaras* for exposing the underbelly of parental turpitude.

Reruns of that show should be used as a warning for young parents on what not to do with their children. But that's a subject for another time. The fact that the show lasted eight seasons on TLC is something of a damning statement on American culture. But amid the depravity of spending thousands of dollars on dresses, costumes, makeup, and hairstyles for girls as young as four years old, there were moments that really stood out.

Like the time one mom dressed her daughter up to look like Dolly Parton, complete with false breasts. If that wasn't enough, there was the six-year-old girl who was dressed up in the famous outfit Julia Roberts styled in the movie *Pretty Woman*.

That's right: black boots, cutoff jean shorts, a white tank top, and a blonde wig. A mother actually dressed up her toddler daughter to look like a hooker from a movie.

To win a beauty contest. Worse, a beauty contest that was held approximately once a week depending on the time of year.

All of which begs the question: What were you thinking?

SPEAKING OF
TODDLERS AND TIARAS

As many of you may remember, *T&T* was also the launching point for Honey Boo Boo, Mama June, and the many incarnations of their television careers (not to mention their time in the tabloids). Perhaps you're thinking that your child (and perhaps yourself) could get in on some of that reality television action and make a small mint.

Sadly (or perhaps gladly), that's not going to be happening for your child and probably not for you, either. Your child is simply not that outspoken or open about her emotions and you don't have any idea the kind of drama that life will create.

Don't be tempted. Take it from Mama June Shannon herself. "It's just not worth the turmoil unless you really don't care."

SHUT UP,
AGE MATTERS

Let's face it, holding your kid back for athletics is stupid. Now, if your *child* is the one who needs a little more academic coaxing, not you, I get it. But you don't want your kid driving themself to baseball practice in the eighth grade.

If they do, it's not really all that impressive when they dominate the fourteen-year-olds they're playing against because they've gone through puberty two years before everyone else.

SHUT UP,
YOUR KID IS NOT GOING TO THE MAJORS ANYTIME SOON

The comment went over like a fart during a sermon.

I was in my midtwenties. It was the 1980s, before I had kids of my own. My best friend, Joey Mitchner, and I were coaching a Little League all-star team and we had a great group of kids. Despite the fact we were coaching in the upper-crust area of Menlo Park, Portola Valley, and Woodside, every one of the kids on the team was terrific.

All good kids who worked hard and listened . . . everything that makes coaching both easy and enjoyable. And trust me, I coached my share of spoiled, insolent kids over the years. What I found most of the time is that those kids come from spoiled, insolent parents. I know you're thinking right now, "Wow, Jason, that's a deep revelation."

Before your sarcasm drips any more, let me also say that there were some parents who were just clueless. There was the one dad who actually came on the field during one game to ask me a question. When I said, "Get off the field, Jack!" I think he honestly felt his health was at risk.

But nothing quite topped what this one dad said on this particular day when Joey and I coached this all-star team. He was the father of the best pitcher on our team. The kid was a strapping lad. Five-foot-eleven and already sporting some heavy peach fuzz by age twelve. As you might expect, he was both imposing and threw hard. While he was a nice kid, he had just enough of a competitive streak to make him really good at that level.

While he was a shoo-in to make the team, we had just spent the better part of a month having some great tryouts for the final squad of fourteen. Between the talent and the attitude of the group, this team had a good chance to compete in the tournament—and did very well, as it turned out.

But on the final night of practices before the tournament, we had the parents come by for a little briefing about what to expect, how the games would be run and, most importantly, about conduct. At the very least, we wanted the parents to feel like we had a plan and that they'd know we were in charge. After decades of coaching and organizing youth sports, I can tell you that there's nothing quite as bad as a disorganized youth sports team to inspire parents to act like their children. We wanted to avoid that at all costs.

As we chatted and talked about various subjects, including how we hoped to get every kid involved in some part of the game so that they felt valued, we had the one dad of the big pitcher who just couldn't keep his mouth shut.

"Well, I guess I'm going to have to figure out how to be an agent when my kid gets older," he said.

Being my sarcastic sportswriter self, it was hard for me to resist mocking the dad. It was the first time I really wanted to say, "Shut up, your kid is not that good." Of course, discretion was the better decision for me, and I still remember the awkward silence. It was somewhere between hearing a belch at the ballet or smelling flatulence in a church pew.

Things got very uncomfortable. I even remember stealing a glance at the son. He looked decidedly uncomfortable with his dad's comment. Not angry or annoyed, just weirdly in the spotlight for no reason.

The truly ironic part was that the dad was perhaps the least athletic person in the group. He was a dumpy older guy who wasn't particularly tall or imposing. His wife was a tall, sturdy woman, so the kid came by his size honestly. The dad was generally nice enough, but just not really clued in when it came to sports.

But at that moment, he couldn't help himself but to say something that basically lived in the reflective glow of his son's talent. All of a sudden, this wonderful team activity was turned into some exercise about individuality. Big Johnny (not the kid's actual name) and his future in the big leagues were about to be put on display instead of this great team activity that kids might remember one day later in life, or even use as a source of pride and motivation for moments that really matter.

And the truly worst part is that the dad couldn't have been more wrong. Sadly for Big Johnny, his size was more of a product of an early growth spurt rather than a straight-line growth. He grew all of one inch from the time he was twelve to when he was a senior in high school. He became a good athlete, getting a couple of all-league and all-region considerations.

Truthfully, baseball wasn't even his best sport by later on. It was just his best sport at the time. Out of all the kids on the team, one of them ended up having a cup of coffee in the minor leagues, and even that was a bit of a surprise to me. While he was one of the better kids on the team, it wasn't like you could tell at age twelve he was going to have that chance.

This is my point when I tell parents to just shut up and enjoy the ride with your kids. If you're going to do anything, help them fall in love with whatever it is that they're doing, whether that's baseball or ballet. Within reason, don't interfere. Don't pretend to know more than you do.

Because, in most cases, you really don't know that much.

BY THE WAY, SHUT UP,

I KNOW MY KID IS NOT GOING PRO IN SOCCER

On the flipside of all this is a notable moment from when I was raising my oldest child. We were at soccer practice one night. Admittedly, my oldest son was not a great athlete. He never loved the competition, and he didn't like to practice, particularly on something that he didn't love in the first place.

However, if you asked him to read or do math problems or discuss physics, he was all in. That's his thing. But when he was younger, I wanted him to at least try some team sports, even if it was just so he could go out there and sweat. Learning about teamwork had value, even if my kid ended up sitting on the bench.

Anyway, one night at soccer practice, one of the moms who was helping coach the co-ed team of six- and seven-year-olds came up to me with her evaluation of my son.

"Dad, it's just not really going to happen for him in the future," said the mom, who had been a horse jockey in her athletic life. I had (and still have) great admiration for the guts and athletic ability it takes to be a jockey. However, I wasn't interested in her evaluation of my son's athletic ability.

That's because I didn't care. My kid wasn't there to become the next Ronaldo or whatever single-named soccer star you came up with. He was just there to learn how to play and have some fun. So, I stared at the mom/coach for a second, thinking about whether to mock her because her kids were never going to be big enough to be more than jockeys.

After a moment to collect my thoughts and decide not to be mean-spirited, I said, "Thanks, I know. It's cool."

SHUT UP,

AND REALIZE THAT ACADEMICS ARE MORE IMPORTANT THAN ATHLETICS

If your kid gets into Harvard but declines so he can play baseball at the University of Miami, it's more likely he'll become a famous business-person than a starting pitcher for the New York Yankees. Don't be a fool; choose Harvard as your school.

SHUT UP
ABOUT YOUR KID SKIPPING A GRADE OR TWO

You may be lucky enough to have an advanced child capable of skipping the second and/or third grade. That's wonderful, but it's really important that you shut up about it. Just understand that your child is going to have a lot of trouble fitting in with children who are more mature physically and possibly emotionally. He or she probably won't be the next Cameron Crowe, writing for *Rolling Stone* at age fifteen.

In other words, it's a wonderful idea to push your kid if they're ready. Just know what you're pushing them into.

SHUT UP,
YOUR KID'S NOT GOING TO BE
THE NEXT CHRIS ROCK

The closest your kid will come to being like Chris Rock is getting slapped in the face for making a joke about the prom queen's bald head.

ALSO,

MAYBE CHECK YOURSELF ON HIM PLAYING
A MOBSTER AT AGE TEN

Speaking of which, just because you're from an Italian family, grew up in New York, and your kid has seen all three *Godfather* movies, *Goodfellas,* and does a good job of saying "lil bit" with the proper inflection at age ten does not mean he's going to be the next Robert DeNiro.

You know what I'm sayin'?

JUST BECAUSE YOUR KID CAN USE
AN EASY-BAKE OVEN,
SHE'S NOT THE NEXT TOP CHEF

Just because your kid makes the best cupcakes in the Easy-Bake oven doesn't mean they're going to be the next Baked by Melissa or pastry chef for Entenmann's. The closest they'll get to a real kitchen is working at Chick-fil-A.

SHUT UP,
YOUR KID IS PROBABLY NOT GOING TO
INFINITY AND BEYOND

Great, your kid knows that Buzz Lightyear is really supposed to be a send-up of Buzz Aldrin. Maybe he or she knows that Aldrin was the second man to step on the moon right after Neil Armstrong and can even recite that famous "One small step" line.

That doesn't make your kid a future astronaut.

Fact is, you're the one in outer space if you think that.

SHUT UP,
WINNING A GAME OF TRIVIAL PURSUIT IS A LONG WAY FROM *JEOPARDY!* CHAMP

Actually, your kid may be so knowledgeable at trivia that you are tempted to take him or her to the Thursday night trivia contest at your favorite bar so that you can win the $50 gift certificate for free nachos and beer. There's certainly high value to that and lots of bragging rights with your bar buddies.

However, that doesn't make him or her the next Ken Jennings, James Holzhauer, or Amy Schneider.

Disclaimer: your child must be twenty-one or older to go to a bar. Please do not get your child a fake ID so you can win trivia night.

SHUT UP,
WINNING THE LOCAL SWIM CONTEST
DOESN'T MAKE YOUR KID . . .

Your kid loves to go to the pool and wins when he or she races against friends. Maybe you even took your kid to swimming lessons at the local YMCA or, if you live in the Fort Lauderdale area, the International Swimming Hall of Fame.

Sorry, your kid is not the next Michael Phelps or Katie Ledecky. Just relax and let them doggie paddle in the shallow end.

SHUT UP,
THE NOBEL PEACE PRIZE IS NOT IN THE MAIL

Your thirteen- or fourteen-year-old child is really interested in the environment and making sure that everyone understands the dangers of global warming. Perhaps he or she stands in front of a capitol building and attracts attention with their ability to speak to the public with great knowledge about a complicated subject. Meanwhile, record-setting temperatures only seem to back up what your kid is saying as she sweats through her speech.

The Nobel Peace Prize is given out every year to people who have done extraordinary things that benefit humans everywhere. Enough said. Unless your kid's name is Greta Thunberg, your kid ain't one of them.

SHUT UP,

YOUR KID IS NOT THE NEXT JIMI HENDRIX
OR EDDIE VAN HALEN

Perhaps your child can string together riffs and power chords to give it a good show and looks great when you pull out your old version of *Guitar Hero*. However, unless he has the amazing hands of Hendrix to envelop a guitar or the pure passion to practice endlessly like Van Halen, just relax before sending him to an agent. The only pick your kid can use is a toothpick.

SHUT UP

AND BE CAREFUL WHAT YOU WISH FOR

Just because your daughter is dramatic at home and enjoys attention, she's not the next Lindsay Lohan—and you probably don't want her to be that.

Unless you want to be the next Michael Lohan.

SHUT UP
AND BE CAREFUL WHAT YOU WISH FOR II

J ust because your six-year-old son can sing and dance very well doesn't mean he's the next Michael Jackson.

And you really don't want him to develop those kinds of issues.

Unless you really are the next Joe Jackson.

SHUT UP
ABOUT YOUR DAUGHTER'S SINGING

Just because your daughter can hit a good high note in the church choir doesn't make her the next Whitney Houston, and she probably won't need a bodyguard.

And don't put that pressure on her.

SHUT UP,
YOUR KID IS NOT GOING TO BE THE FACE OF
THE NEXT BIG COOKING SHOW

O kay, your daughter may be cute and know how to cook a little. She's not going to be the next media personality to win the Food Network's *Kids Baking Championship* or survive the cloche on *Chopped Junior.*

SHUT UP,
YOUR KID IS NOT THE NEXT MARTIN SCORSESE
OR STEVEN SPIELBERG

Just because your kid made a couple of cool TikTok videos by age eight and really understands the message of *Get Shorty* when you all watched it on family night does not mean he or she is going to be the next great Hollywood director.

Plus, do you really want him or her to make something as tired as *The Irishman*?

SHUT UP,
YOUR KID IS NOT
THE NEXT GREAT MARATHON RUNNER

Okay, your ten-year-old kid just blew away his age group and even a bunch of adult runners at the local 5K race (or maybe even a 10K). He's still not going to become the next great marathon runner. Unless you immediately send him to train in the mountains of Kenya.

SHUT UP,
YOUR KID IS NOT
THE NEXT ELON MUSK

Do you know that next-door neighbor of yours who has the really dumb parents but gets straight As? There's a very good chance they won't be the next Elon Musk, but they might be his kid.

SHUT UP,
YOUR KID IS NOT A GENIUS JUST BECAUSE
THEY CAN READ BY AGE TWO

Just because your kid started reading the *New York Times* at age two doesn't make them any smarter than the kid who started reading the *New York Post* at age six.

SHUT UP,
YOUR DAUGHTER IS NOT
THE NEXT SIMONE BILES

Okay, your child rolled over in her cradle at three months of age and has amazing body control. There's a long way between that and being one of the greatest gymnasts in the history of the world.

And is your daughter really only going to be four-foot-eight to possess that kind of body control?

SHUT UP,
YOUR KID IS NOT GOING TO BE
THE NEXT MOODY ARTIST

G ranted, a lot of kids out there are disaffected and distant from you as teenagers. As a parent, you're having a hard time connecting with them, even though they are super creative and have a good singing voice.

It doesn't mean they are the next Billie Eilish.

SHUT UP,
YOUR KID'S NOT
THE NEXT BOB ROSS

Just because your child got an A in art class for their amazing land-scape doesn't mean they're going to paint those happy trees like Bob Ross, RIP.

SHUT UP,
YOUR KID'S NOT GOING TO BE
A CIA AGENT

Sure, a lot of kids' dream is to be a spy like Inspector Gadget or Kim Possible. If you're not careful, the closest your kid is going to get to being a CIA agent is stalking their ex on Facebook, Instagram, or LinkedIn—or any social media platform that's created after this book is published.

SHUT UP,
YOUR KID IS NOT
THE NEXT GREAT DIVA

Okay, your kid has swagger like no other, carries herself with a sense of confidence that few humans can even imagine, and has no problem strutting her stuff on stage. She's still a long way from being Beyonce, fully equipped with a lemonade stand and a beehive. She's probably not even Jennifer Lopez or the Queen of Soul herself, Aretha Franklin.

ALSO,
LET YOUR CHILD GROW UP

Look, it's always cool to look young, but there comes a point when your child needs to realize she's not sixteen years old anymore and isn't a little pixie waiting to be asked out to the prom by the captain of the football team.

Let's say by age twenty-nine, it's time to start acting like, you know, an adult.

Even Miley Cyrus eventually let go of Hannah Montana.

SHUT UP,
YOUR KID'S HYPERACTIVITY IS
NOT NECESSARILY TALENT

J ust because your kid is funny, quick-witted, and bounces off the walls like a Super Ball in a high-school gymnasium does not mean that he or she will be the next Robin Williams.

Although we sure could use another one.

SHUT UP,
YOUR KID IS NOT READY TO RUMBLE

We all know that sports need more than just great athletes, but also good hype men along the way. That guy who gets the crowd ready to go by screaming some version of, "Are you ready to RUM-MMMMMMBBBLLLLLE?" is important in his own way. So is a great announcer, play-by-play guy, or analyst.

But just because your kid is a sports fan, knows every piece of sports trivia in the world, and can talk about sports all day doesn't mean he's going to be the next Jim Nantz, Joe Buck, Tony Romo, or the legendary Vin Scully.

SHUT UP

AND GET OUT OF THE WAY OF YOUR SON'S CAREER

Outside of the likes of Jay-Z and Kendrick Lamar, the shelf life of a rapper is roughly the length of a mayfly. Most are lucky to get hot for three or four years before they are, as the saying goes, "cold product." See the case of one Atlanta-area rapper who will go unnamed, because this recording executive felt so bad about what happened to him.

His dad redefined the idea of moving the goalposts.

"Every time we thought we had a deal, the dad changed what he wanted," the recording executive said. "At first, he was totally unrealistic about how much he could get for an advance. We were offering a hundred thousand dollars and the dad kept demanding three hundred thousand dollars. There was just no way we, or anybody else, was going to do that."

With each turn in the negotiations, the father wanted something different, and it was usually so ridiculous that the executives in charge of the decision didn't know how to react. If the dad agreed to take less on the advance, he would want a percentage on the backside that would make it nearly impossible for the recording company to make money.

"He just didn't understand how the business worked. His son was going to make millions if he was just reasonably successful. But (the dad) was scared that he was somehow getting taken . . . really, he just should have hired an agent," the executive said.

The other problem the dad didn't seem to get was that the clock was ticking. His son had become big on the club circuit. The crowds loved the rhymes, but that's about as important as being the latest thing on social media.

One day you're hotter than Facebook in 2004. The next day you're about as cool as Mark Zuckerberg using SPF ten million in 2021.

From the time of the first offer to when the young rapper signed, the process took more than three years. The rapper's time in the sun was pretty much done.

"Millions, just gone because of the missed opportunity."

SHUT UP,

YOUR KID IS NOT THE SECOND COMING

can't take credit for this tidbit. It comes from a 2018 article on Healthyway.com and it is simply too good to pass up. The article was a series of stories from teachers who had to deal with parents. This one happened to be from a kindergarten teacher. The teacher relayed the basics of a conversation she had with one mom.

The mother said to the teacher that "she was told by their church prophet that my student was sent to lead the world into salvation." Aside from the immediate question of whether the church prophet was somehow trying to make a profit on the mother by buttering up the family, the stated prophecy set up all sorts of questions about what might happen if the child fell somewhat short of that goal. Is being simply an apostle acceptable?

If the child only gets to be pope, does that suffice?

Beyond that, what do you teach a future savior if you're the kindergarten teacher? Is *Green Eggs and Ham* a good first book, or does the teacher have to go straight to the Book of Genesis? It is definitely a quandary.

SHUT UP

AND WEAR A SUIT TO A BUSINESS MEETING

When Reggie Bush lost his Heisman Trophy at the University of Southern California for taking more than $300,000 in illicit benefits, he and his family weren't exactly super secretive about being on the take. In fact, they were comically obvious, starting with the fact that his mother and stepfather, Lamar Griffin, somehow moved from a one-bedroom apartment into a $750,000 home during Bush's senior year.

When reporters came to the house to verify that the family lived there, it didn't take much effort. The family had put their name in the cement of the driveway.

Bush's parents were also demanding their share of the take. Aside from things like hotel rooms at the Ritz Carlton in San Francisco and an all-expense paid trip to Hawaii for a game, the father had big dreams of becoming something more than a security guard at a San Diego–area high school. Griffin posed an idea to one of the marketing agents who was a member of the powerful Sycuan Tribe, which operated a casino.

Griffin wanted to be in charge of security for the entire casino.

Out of respect for Griffin (and in hopes of keeping the family happy), the tribe invited Griffin to come to a meeting of the Tribal Council to pitch his idea.

Griffin showed up wearing a No. 5 USC replica jersey of the one Bush wore at USC. Suffice to say, the two sides never struck a deal.

SHUT UP,
YOUR KID DOESN'T GET PAID FOR COLLEGE STATS

Going into the 1994 NFL Draft, Ronnie Woolfork and his family had high hopes. Woolfork had stumbled a bit as a senior, dropping to only 6.5 sacks that season after getting a combined 26.5 in his sophomore and junior seasons.

Woolfork had gained a bit of weight as a senior, tipping in at more than 250 pounds. But that was hardly much of a problem. Hope still ran high that he'd get picked in the second or third round. Woolfork ended up in the fourth, getting selected by the Miami Dolphins, who desperately needed pass rushers. If Woolfork had even a hint of ability to get to the quarterback, he would have made the team.

Instead, Woolfork showed up at an offseason camp and was so mediocre that the Dolphins withdrew their original contract offer. They realized quickly that Woolfork was both too heavy and, in reality, he was the beneficiary of playing around a lot of talented teammates in college.

The new deal included no signing bonus, which was virtually unheard of. If that wasn't enough of an indication of what the Dolphins felt, there was their indifference when Woolfork held out at the beginning of training camp.

That's when his father decided to get involved. Against the advice of his agent, Woolfork's father rented a room at a hotel near the Dolphins training facility, invited the press to the event, and made the issue a public matter.

As if legendary Dolphins coach Don Shula was going to worry about what a dad had to say.

Anyway, the spectacle turned into a rant. After a few minutes of explaining the situation, Woolfork's father started yelling to the reporters, "Look at the stats!" He alternated that by discussing how he and his kid were part of the "Wolf Pack," a play on their last name.

The Dolphins were unmoved. As things turned out, Woolfork never played for Miami. He ended up playing as a backup for four games for Kansas City the following years, then ended up playing in Europe for a couple of seasons.

Certainly nothing to be embarrassed about, but a long way from his father's bellicose declarations.

SHUT UP,
YOUR KID IS NOT
THE NEXT YOU

Don Shula ended up as the winningest coach in NFL history. He also couldn't help himself when it came to the coaching careers of both of his sons, David and Mike. David was a study in nepotism that ultimately undermined his overall ability to learn the job.

After graduating from Dartmouth and playing one year in the NFL with Baltimore in 1981, David became an assistant coach under his father with the Miami Dolphins. David spent seven years as an assistant coach under his famed father, which shielded him from much of the criticism foisted upon him by the likes of star quarterback Dan Marino and wide receivers Mark Duper and Mark Clayton. David was regularly mocked by those three when he tried to institute drills that they found silly.

Instead of learning how to convince players about the benefits of what he was teaching, David became obstinate. So did his famous father, who eventually pushed David to become the offensive coordinator with the Dallas Cowboys under Jimmy Johnson in 1989 and 1990.

When that didn't work, Johnson had to fire David Shula, creating a rift between the elder Shula and Johnson that never healed. David returned to Miami for a year and his father used his connections to the family of Bengals owner Mike Brown to get David the head coaching job in Cincinnati in 1992. Don had played for Brown's legendary father Paul Brown.

David's five disastrous seasons with the Bengals were painful to watch, ending with a 19-52 record and not a single winning season. But the run of bad years was essentially presaged in his first season.

During a Monday night game on October 19, 1992, between Cincinnati and Pittsburgh in which the Bengals got shut out, the younger Shula had a sideline confrontation with veteran linebacker Gary Reasons. It was an obvious attempt by David to show who was boss on national TV, in front of his whole team, and to the Bengals fan base.

Little Shula picked the wrong guy. Reasons had spent the previous eight years of his career with the New York Giants, had won two Super Bowl rings as part of one of the greatest defenses in NFL history, and had been coached by Bill Parcells, a man who played Alpha male games like no coach in the history of the league.

As David shouted at Reasons, the moment looked more like a faceoff with Goliath. Reasons didn't hit Shula. He did something much worse.

He tugged on the bill of Shula's cap, making Shula look like a little boy.

"My first reaction was to laugh," said Mike Westhoff, a longtime Dolphins assistant coach. "Then I caught myself and thought, if that was Don, he would have cut Reasons right there on the sideline. David just took it. It was awful. You can't do that in this game. Players smell fear."

SHUT UP,
YOUR KID IS NOW IN COLLEGE

I t's not completely unusual for parents to monitor their children's progress in college. It's something different for a parent to monitor the progress of individual professors.

"I had one parent who called to complain about her son's grades," the late Diane Middlebrook said during her career as a professor of feminist studies at Stanford. "His work was pretty typical, but his mother thought I had it out for him because he was from a conservative family."

The son's father was a judge in the family's hometown. So, the mother thought Middlebrook had checked out the son's background and had it out for the son. The mother started complaining to Middlebrook, talking about Middlebrook's feminist leanings and how that likely impacted her political view.

"It was somewhat amusing because she quoted back some of my work to me and told me how I must have read some of her husband's court rulings. She really did do a lot of reading about me. No matter how much I talked to her about her son, it didn't matter. The mom thought it was a plot. Finally, I just said, 'Ma'am, I don't even know who your husband is,' and she finally shut up."

Middlebrook, who passed away in 2007, chuckled about the whole thing and recalled how it ended with the student coming to her office one day, apologizing for his mother's behavior.

"I told him not to worry about it. Before he left, he said, 'I just wish my mom would take this class and learn something.'"

SHUT UP,
YOUR REPUTATION HURTS YOUR KID

In another case of nepotism gone wrong, there's the story of the former boy band member who eventually had a son who wanted to get into country music.

There was just one hitch: The former boy band member had been an incredibly high-maintenance performer during his days in the business. Or, to put it bluntly, "He was just an asshole," as one executive said.

When it came time to ask for some favors as his son tried to develop his career, no one was ready to step forward.

"I don't think the kid was ever going to make it," the executive said. "But he sure wasn't going to get help based on his dad."

SHUT UP,
YOUR KID IS TALENTED IN OTHER WAYS

The father of Skylar Astin never really liked to listen. As his famous son was preparing for a singing career on Broadway in musicals such as *Pitch Perfect* and in other live venues around the world, Astin's father was trying to convince agents and music executives that his son had a future as a pop singer.

One after one, those agents and executives said that Astin would have a great career in theater, which had turned out to be true.

"But it was like the dad got offended," one agent said. "Even two years after, when his son was starring on Broadway, he was still pissed. He just had it so set in his mind."

SHUT UP.

NO REALLY, YOU NEED TO JUST SHUT UP

O nce upon a time early in Connor Cook's career at Michigan State, there were scouts who believed he might one day become a first-round draft pick. At 6-foot-4 and 225 pounds, Cook had the prototypical size and measurable skills that made him look like a great prospect.

Cook had just two problems: His teammates didn't think he was much of a leader and his dad Chris was a complete pain in the ass.

The story among people associated with the Michigan State program is that Cook did all sorts of things to alienate himself from his teammates. That included not showing up for offseason workouts on campus when other players devoted their summers to getting better and building camaraderie on the team. Among some of the things that annoyed teammates most was that Cook would post pictures of himself on social media hanging out at his family's summer home on a lake while his teammates were back at Michigan State working out.

To little surprise, Cook was not voted as a captain for his senior season. This was like something straight out of the movie *Draft Day* with Kevin Costner, only it was real. That's when Cook's father Chris started to get involved. Chris Cook went to Michigan State coach Mark Dantonio to complain about his son not being a captain.

When word of Chris Cook going to Dantonio got to NFL scouts during Cook's senior season, there was a collective eye roll.

"A bunch of us were out to dinner one night before a game," one NFL scout said. "We all knew about the dad because so many people at Michigan State hated him . . . I can't remember who said it, but one of us just blurted out, 'It tells you all you need to know that the dad went to Dantonio instead of just talking to his son.' The dad wasn't even a leader."

That was just the beginning. Beyond his father's interference, Connor Cook was very active on social media, including his tendency to send out homophobic tweets and get into fights with reporters online.

"There were two big problems with Connor Cook. First, he was a [jerk]. Super arrogant and aloof," the scout said. "But the second problem is that his dad was worse. Connor didn't have any leadership skills because his father was even worse."

Cook and his father were such jerks that they even annoyed Raiders coach Jon Gruden, who had once claimed before the 2016 draft that he thought Cook should have been a first-round pick.

"Star quarterback in the Big Ten," Gruden once said, growling at a reporter. "You see that kid's stats? I'll take him all day." Except that when Gruden took over as head coach of the Raiders in 2018, he let Cook go after hearing from the other players.

SHUT UP,
YOU'RE NOT KING RICHARD

The movie *King Richard*, which tells the story of father Richard Williams and his support for daughters Venus and Serena, created quite a stir that went beyond Will Smith winning an Oscar and feeling the gumption to deliver the slap heard 'round the world.

For one tennis coach in the Los Angeles area, it led to a number of parents feeling very courageous about what they were willing to say to him.

"I had one parent who was yelling at me about how his ten-year-old daughter should be playing up at a higher level, against twelve-year-old girls. He must have watched that movie every day before practice. This went on for three weeks. I kept telling the dad that his daughter wasn't even close to being ready for that. She wasn't even the best ten-year-old in the group," the coach said.

"Finally, I had enough and said I'd arrange a match between his daughter and another girl who was the lowest-ranked twelve-year-old," the coach said. "His daughter didn't win a point. She never held serve one time. Just a runover. I felt bad because I thought the daughter would lose confidence, but she was fine. Fortunately, I haven't heard from the dad again."

SHUT UP

AND DON'T TALK TO YOUR KID WHILE HE'S HITTING

Former Major League Baseball player Eric Byrnes was passionate from the word go. As a Little Leaguer, Byrnes would climb fences in pursuit of flyballs, stomp around the mound as a pitcher to bring himself to full intensity, and even once dropped to his knees in tears when he struck out with the bases loaded.

In short, Byrnes always played like his hair was on fire. To his parents' credit, they never did anything to quell that passion, which served him well. In fact, Byrnes' father would often watch games while leaning on the centerfield fence, smiling at every bit of his son's passionate histrionics.

After Byrnes retired from baseball and became a parent, he started coaching youth baseball on some of the better travel ball teams. As you might imagine, he ended up working with talented kids and, in turn, parents who were pretty intense. Fortunately, his resume as a former major leaguer kept the parents in check and Byrnes' dedication to keeping the game fun kept the kids happy.

But there was one moment that jumped off the page as a little weird even to the hyper Byrnes. During a game, one of the dads started talking to his son in the middle of the at-bat. In turn, the son started arguing with his dad.

"They're actually going through this whole discussion of what's happening during the at-bat as the kid is standing there at the plate waiting for the next pitch," Byrnes said. "It was really kind of bizarre and I didn't know what to say. But it was kind of a typical father-son argument, so it was kind of pretty in its own way. I told the dad that wasn't probably the best way to handle it, but I think he already realized that before I said anything."

SHUT UP

AND DON'T YELL AT THE REFS . . .
ESPECIALLY IF YOU DON'T KNOW THE RULES

I was coaching youth basketball in my twenties when I showed up early for a game. Another game was already in progress. A young group of kids—roughly eight- and nine-year-olds—were playing and, as often happens, the game was a little lopsided.

One of the dads from the team that was losing started yelling at the coach of his child's team, demanding that the team play zone defense to keep the other team from scoring so easily. The coach was a really young guy, probably still in high school. He was flummoxed and didn't know how to respond.

During a stoppage in play, the dad yelled for zone defense for roughly the third time. The referee shouted to the dad, "You can't play zone defense, it's man to man only so your kid actually learns how to play defense."

The dad sat down.

SHUT UP

AND LET YOUR KID DECIDE

I n 2013, Andrea McDonald turned National Signing Day into a chase scene out of a comedy-action movie. McDonald is the mother of Alex Collins, a running back who eventually played in the NFL and, at the time, was one of the top backs in the country coming out of South Plantation High in Florida.

Since South Plantation was only a short drive from the University of Miami, historically one of the best college programs in the country, Collins was leaning heavily toward playing there, which met with great approval from his mother. However, Collins, like many players, changed his mind and decommitted from Miami and was set to sign with the University of Arkansas.

The plan was for Collins to sign his letter of intent with Arkansas at his high school on National Signing Day. Local TV stations and newspaper reporters from various South Florida outlets showed up at the school. There was just one problem; McDonald had snuck into the high school earlier in the day and stolen the letter of intent, which she was also supposed to sign as his parent.

Collins went looking for his mother, but she couldn't be found. The story turned into something of a circus with ESPN reporters trying to explain on-air that the mother had absconded with the paperwork. The running back's mom was on the loose.

Collins had to get his father to sign the paperwork instead of his mother, allowing him to go to Arkansas, where he had a successful career. However, the story wasn't done at that point. His mother, still hoping to control the situation, hired the law firm founded by the late Johnny Cochran in an attempt to assert her rights (not that she had any). Cochran was better known for his successful defense of a much more infamous running back, O.J. Simpson.

SHUT UP
AND DON'T SING

This was another fun story from Healthyway.com's 2018 article on overwrought parents and came from a music teacher.

"I had a mother of a student who would crash choir rehearsal for our Christmas concert and try to 'demonstrate' how she had learned to sing 'O Holy Night' when she had been a student," the teacher wrote. "Not only was her pitch three cents short of a dollar, but it took the principal and custodian to escort her out of the rehearsal room. For their part, the students thought it was 'planned comedy.' However, it was not."

SHUT UP
AND DON'T BE LAVAR BALL

aVar Ball is something of a legend in the world of interfering parents, although two of his sons are in the NBA and his youngest son LaMelo was the NBA Rookie of the Year in 2021 and an NBA All-Star in 2022.

However, the elder Ball has spent most of his sons' careers writing checks with his mouth that he could never cash, including saying things like how he could have beaten LeBron James one-on-one in his prime.

But the biggest check Daddy Ball wrote wrong was in 2017 when he announced that he was starting a shoe and apparel company called Big Baller Brand with his oldest son Lonzo as the face of the company. Lonzo had just been selected with the No. 2 overall pick in the NBA Draft by his hometown Los Angeles Lakers.

The buzz was supposed to be huge and even famous entertainment moguls like Jay-Z were impressed by the aggressiveness.

There was just one problem. They didn't really know how to make shoes or clothing and they absolutely didn't know how to distribute merchandise. LaVar put in millions of his own money to support the company and the company even got some minor celebrities, such as NBA guard Jordan Crawford and rapper Quavo, to endorse the brand.

However, the company was lambasted by complaints from customers who either didn't get the right products they ordered, didn't get them for weeks or months, or didn't get anything at all. Major League Baseball player Adam Jones went on social media in 2018 to say that he hadn't received anything even after a year following his order. The Better Business Bureau gave Big Baller Brand an F grade.

Worse for LaVar Ball, he reportedly lost $1.5 million in the venture, which ended in a flurry of lawsuits.

SHUT UP,
YOUR KID IS NOT A SCIENCE EXPERIMENT

Marv Marinovich was a man ahead of his time.

Marinovich was one of the first strength and conditioning coaches in the NFL. He got his start with famed Oakland Raiders owner Al Davis, who had met Marinovich when Marinovich was an offensive lineman and Davis was an assistant coach at the University of Southern California.

Davis loved Marinovich as a player because he was high energy and driven in a William Wallace kind of way. As a senior at USC, he was named the Most Inspirational Player in a vote by his teammates. If you needed someone to charge at the opponent with nothing but a shield and a sword while screaming like a banshee and flashing a terrifying look on his face, Marinovich was your guy.

He was like something out of central casting in Hollywood. He was the grandson of a Croatian immigrant farmer on his father's side who was a former member of the Russian army. Legend has it that

Marinovich's grandfather was so intense that he supervised the surgery to have his arm amputated after it was severely injured in battle.

Yes, the Marinovich Family was very much, as the saying goes, touched by a passion that bordered on lunacy.

Anyway, Marinovich was in the sports training business long before it was considered a real thing. He did some very serious study on Eastern Bloc methods, such as speed training and how to make athletes more explosive. He didn't just study workout routines, he studied diet and sleep patterns, and plenty of those close to him claim he dabbled in steroids in the 1960s.

On July 4, 1969, Marinovich and his first wife had son Todd—and dad had a plan. He was going to turn his son into the greatest quarterback in the history of the planet. The process started almost from Day 1, as *Sports Illustrated* noted in a story on Todd when he was playing quarterback at his father's alma mater.

"When Todd was one month old, Marv was already working on his son's physical conditioning. He stretched his hamstrings. Pushups were next. Marv invented a game in which Todd would try to lift a medicine ball onto a kitchen counter. Marv also put him on a balance beam. Both activities grew easier when Todd learned to walk. There was a football in Todd's crib from day one. 'Not a real NFL ball,' says Marv. 'That would be sick; it was a stuffed ball.'"

Marinovich also claimed that his son had followed a superstrict diet all his life. That included never having eaten a Big Mac, an Oreo, or a Ding Dong. Dad even claimed that when his son went to birthday parties for his friends, the family would bring Todd's own cake and ice cream to avoid sugar and refined white flour. He ate homemade condiments, unprocessed dairy, and all-natural, hormone-free beef. Todd confirmed all of it.

There was just one problem with the story: It was a lie that got out of control. His maternal grandparents would buy him junk food when he was in elementary school, and the only reason the story kept its legs is that Todd was too afraid to face up to Marv, who had a violent temper. By the time Todd was in college, he had friends who would buy him Big Macs and other fast food.

"The whole thing about him never having a Big Mac was a total joke," one classmate said years later. "He ate all that stuff and he couldn't stand what his dad was doing."

The problem is that Todd was secretly willful instead of simply standing up to his dad, who by later in their lives had become basically impossible to live with. Marinovich's wife divorced him, and he and Todd ended up living in a one-bedroom apartment when Todd was in high school. Serious problems started to show up when Todd was playing for the Trojans in 1990. He skipped classes in college, got into on-field yelling matches with coach Larry Smith, and after the season was arrested for cocaine possession.

Todd was still good enough to get drafted in the first round by Davis and the Raiders in 1991. However, his drug use and obstinate behavior continued to spiral until he was out of the NFL after three years, having made more than $2 million in his brief career. Marinovich eventually ended up playing in a rock band after bouncing around the Canadian Football League and other minor football leagues. He also painted, opened his own art gallery, battled addiction his entire life, and bounced through numerous relationships.

Sadly, there isn't much humor to this story, except for some self-deprecating jokes. One time at a USC practice Todd was attending years after his college career, he was joking with some players and coaches about how to stay healthy. Even into his forties, Todd was in great physical condition despite his travails. That didn't go unnoticed by the group.

That's when Todd quipped: "Don't be afraid to have a Big Mac."

SHUT UP

AND DON'T COME ON THE FIELD DURING A GAME

As a youth coach, I always liked to have the parents of the kids on the team ask me as many questions as possible. First, I always wanted them to understand the reason I did whatever I was trying to do. Second, I never wanted them to think I was hiding anything from them. It was really about basic trust.

That led to some great conversations over the years. There was the one mom who told me how disappointed her son was that he wasn't the starting pitcher on the Little League team I coached. His name was Mark, and he always pitched the fourth, fifth, and sixth innings for us.

As I explained to the mom, the reason had nothing to do with talent. It was just about logic. Jess, the kid who was the starting pitcher and was on the mound for the first three innings, was also our best catcher. I wanted Jess to pitch before he caught so he wasn't tired out from catching in the first part of the game. After I explained it to the mom, I explained it to Mark and he never had another problem.

But there were some parents who didn't quite know how to ask straightforward questions. Or, more specifically, when to ask those questions. In the middle of a game as I was trying to coach the game was not the right time.

That's what one parent attempted to do one day. He was a parent of the best pitcher on our team, a tall, lanky kid who threw very hard. Unfortunately, he had a little Nuke LaLoosh to him. There were times when he couldn't find the strike zone if it were on a map. The secret with him was trying to find a consistent release point and hope the muscle memory would take over.

On this one day, his muscles were overwhelmed by amnesia. If there had been a man dressed in a bull outfit, there would have been a first-inning knockout. As he continued to struggle and I tried to think of some way to get him in a groove, I heard a voice over my right shoulder.

The kid's dad had walked onto the field and wanted to ask me a question about what was going on with his son. Now, it would have been one thing if this were a dad who helped out with the coaching and showed up on a regular basis. This dad never so much as lifted a catcher's mask.

Within a millisecond I knew that I couldn't have this. If I allowed one parent to come on the field, I would never have any control of the team, whether that was with the parents or the kids. Without thinking, I said in a stern tone, "Jack, get off the field."

The dad was caught off guard but tried to finish his question. He got half a word out before I said, "Jack, get OFF the field," in a loud enough voice that everybody started to look. The dad started to get unnerved at that point, put up his hands, and tried one more time to open his mouth to finish the question.

I just stood my ground, pointed toward the gate to get off the field, and said in a slightly louder voice, "Jack, I said get OFF THE FIELD." At that point, the dad scurried away. I turned back toward the game, glancing at the stands where the other parents were sitting. There was a combination of fear and humor in the eyes of the other parents.

I had to establish who was boss.

After the game, Jack the dad went up to my best friend (and fellow coach) and asked if I was under some kind of stress. That became a running gag between us. Every time we saw Jack show up for a game after that, my friend would ask if I was feeling stressed and I'd tell him to get off the field.

SHUT UP
AND LEARN ABOUT GENETICS

The last class story that was unearthed by Healthyway.com was about a mother of twins. The teacher explained that she had a pair of twins in her French class.

"One was quite bright, but not perfect; say in the B-plus to A-minus range. The other, not so much. The other twin was failing by a large margin."

On Parents' Night, the mother came to the class and discussed the performance of her children. "We all talk about the first twin's grades. I'm mainly saying that they do this well, and this, and that they need to work on this to get past the B-plus. As for the other twin, we list our concerns: They are good at this, but they really struggle with that, blah blah blah. Just your standard feedback that would help both twins do well."

Then the mother gave a staggering response that left the teacher speechless.

"You'd think her comment was a joke, but she was serious—dead serious. And I bet it's not the first time she's said it. Her response: 'But if they're identical twins, shouldn't they have the same grade?'"

SHUT UP
AND DON'T COME TO THE GAME UNINVITED

There are plenty of stories about parents who walked out on their children only to return years later after their sons or daughters hit it big in whatever they did. For instance, Colin Kaepernick, Reggie Bush, and Michael Vick all had mothers and/or fathers who were basically out of their lives for years, only to resurface when they were in college or the pros.

The worst tries at reunions are the "blind date" attempts that often happen. The estranged parent shows up at a game and tries to get the attention of their child before a game. Normally, this goes over like a storm cloud in a hurricane. There are a lot of rough emotions that athletes suddenly deal with at a time when they are trying to focus on winning a game.

But there was one athlete who rolled with the situation with unusual aplomb, although he never talked about it publicly because he didn't want to embarrass his father more than he did at that moment.

"He tried to say, 'Son, can we talk?' I was like, 'Sure, can I bring you in the locker room and introduce you to all my teammates and coaches before the game? Maybe after I explain I haven't seen you for twenty years, the coaches will want to tell you about the game plan.' After I invited him to ride back on the team plane, I think he got the full idea of how sarcastic I was being," the player said.

"The good part is that he took it in the spirit intended. He wrote me later and apologized and we worked it out. He actually laughed about how sarcastic I was that day. He said it reminded him of himself."

SHUT UP
AND DON'T TURN YOUR KID INTO A VAGABOND

If you talk to enough college and professional coaches, you will hear horror about having to deal with what many of them call the "vagabond syndrome" in team sports. It's young athletes who have no real sense of community or, more specifically, no ability to interact with other people.

And perhaps no athlete ever represented that better than Perry Klein, who once upon a time seemed destined for stardom as a quarterback. He also was a great volleyball player who was considered a scholarship athlete in both sports.

Then he started going on a tour of schools in hopes of propping up his own status.

"I'm not going to say he was the worst athlete I ever coached in terms of communication, but for a quarterback he was way off at the bad end of the spectrum," said Darrel "Mouse" Davis, a former quarterback coach with the Atlanta Falcons. "You have to be able to talk to people and he just couldn't do it."

After being a fourth-round pick in 1994, and highly touted as an excellent athlete, Klein played only three years in the NFL and threw exactly one pass. This is a guy who once set a California high school record by completing 46 of 49 passes in a game, quarterbacked powerhouse Carson High to the Los Angeles City championship, was named the State Player of the Year, the LA Player of the Year, and a *Parade* All-American.

So, what happened?

"He was only ever in it for himself," a former NFL executive said. "It wasn't about being on a team, it was about being on a team that helped promote the idea of Perry Klein."

The championship at Carson was a perfect example. After playing at Palisades High in an affluent part of LA where he grew up, Klein transferred to Carson, which was in one of the roughest parts of the city at the time. Klein's family claimed they had moved there. It was a farce. Klein played the season and then immediately transferred back to Palisades.

As people in LA recalled, it ultimately made Klein look very bad. Instead of being revered, he was essentially hated by people at two different schools. The situation didn't improve much in college. After playing three years at the University of California at Berkeley, Klein transferred to C.W. Post in New York.

"It's funny to look back on," said the late Gary Wichard, who was Klein's agent. "The sport he really was best at was volleyball. It was because he fit in with all those guys and was comfortable. He was never comfortable in football."

SHUT UP

AND JUST ENJOY IT WHEN YOUR KID RUINS
THE CHRISTMAS RECITAL

One of my favorite stories is about my youngest son Campbell, who was quite the rapscallion when he was young. When he was four years old, he pulled a little number at the First Presbyterian preschool Christmas pageant. Instead of just singing along with the song, he took the advice of his older brother and decided to hit the "dead button" in the middle of the song and simply lay on the floor.

This pushed his teacher, Miss Janet, to distraction as she tried to lift him by one arm without damaging his elf outfit. He didn't cooperate and poor Janet wasn't strong enough to get him upright. It was quite good and got most of the parents laughing during an otherwise cliché kids' event.

Despite his mother giving him a good talking-to after that event, Campbell didn't relent. In fact, the following Christmas pageant was a showstopper.

Campbell and the rest of his preschool classmates were dressed in Santa hats and green vests. Shortly after the song began, Campbell led three other classmates on a march around the stage. The teachers, fully expecting some shenanigans from my recalcitrant child, were able to corral the other three children as they circled the lectern on the stage of the church.

Alertly, Campbell escaped into the choir pews and headed toward the organ in the middle of the pews, setting off a roar of laughter from the parents that only fueled Campbell's mischievousness. As he was chased by his latest teacher—whose name I can't recall all these years later—his escape route was cut off by the director of the preschool.

Realizing he was out of options, Campbell didn't go quietly. He looked back at the crowd and tilted his head to flash an ear-to-ear grin that stole the show and earned gigantic applause. Even his mother, who read him the riot act before the preschool graduation in the spring, couldn't resist at the moment.

But I'll say this for Campbell's efforts: He has never been afraid to put himself on stage since that day. When stuff like that happens, shut up and let it happen.

SHUT UP,
YOUR KID'S NOT
THE NEXT KARDASHIAN

Whether the *goal* is to be the next Kim or to be the second coming of Khloe, just don't do it. Please, don't do it.

Unless you really are as manipulative as Kris.

SHUT UP,
YOUR KID'S NOT
THE NEXT ALBERT EINSTEIN

S ure, your kid won the science fair by making a glass of milk some-how pump air into a balloon. While a great experiment, don't ever compare him to the GOAT of science and the creator of $e=mc^2$.

SHUT UP,
YOUR KID'S NOT
THE NEXT NASCAR SUPERSTAR

Just because your kid knows how to ride a quad and is great with go-karts doesn't mean they're going to be able to ride around in circles for four hours while holding in their urine.

And eventually, you're going to want them to learn how to turn right.

SHUT UP,
YOUR KID'S NOT GOING TO BE
THE NEXT SPELLING BEE CHAMPION

Maybe you're like me and you used to help your kid work on his spelling test on the way to and from school by making flip cards from 3x5 index cards. Maybe you even helped your kid learn certain mnemonics, such as "'I' before 'E' except after 'C.'"

Maybe your child is smart enough to remember how to spell "mnemonics." Maybe you've read about how former Spelling Bee champions have become lawyers and doctors and achieve all sorts of successes.

But do you really want your kid doing nothing but memorizing words and rules so that they can be seen on TV standing up and reciting words? Is that really a goal? Are you trying to raise the next Steve Urkel?

SHUT UP,
YOUR KID'S NOT
THE NEXT KANYE WEST

So maybe your kid is really good at poetry and can piece together some lyrics that have a little zest. Maybe he even quotes some of Ye's best lines (many of which seem to come out of a self-help book), such as, "Living well eliminates the need for revenge."

But as we (and Pete Davidson, especially) know, there is a neurotic, self-absorbed, and entitled side to West. Take a sample from Kim K. and say no to the Ye.

SHUT UP,
YOUR KID'S NOT
THE NEXT RYAN'S WORLD

Not every kid can compel millions of other kids to watch them open toys on YouTube. Let your kid's unboxing videos happen on their birthday.

And let them do it in privacy with a little dignity.

SHUT UP,
YOUR KID'S NOT
THE NEXT SUPERMODEL

Unless you really hope that your daughter will go the next fifteen years without eating a slice of pizza or that your son will learn to live without carbs for most of his life, that career in modeling is pretty much a longshot.

Instead, turn on *America's Next Top Model* and call it a day. Just ask Barry Williams.

SHUT UP,
YOUR KID'S NOT GOING TO BE
THE NEXT DARCI LYNNE

Okay, your kid has some talent by age twelve, including the ability to sing and maybe even tell a joke. But ventriloquism, too? Come on. And stage presence? Look, even if your kid is great, he or she is not going to get the next golden buzzer on *America's Got Talent*.

SHUT UP,
YOUR KID'S NOT GOING TO BE
THE NEXT CECELIA CASSINI

While your kid knows how to dress up her American Doll and watches every season of *Project Runway,* there's only one kid selling designs to Taylor Swift and Heidi Klum, and your kid's not the Mozart of fashion.

SHUT UP,
YOUR KID'S NOT GOING TO BE
THE NEXT REALITY STAR

Frankly, should becoming the next Snooki or The Situation be a goal?

SHUT UP,
YOUR KID'S NOT GOING TO BE
THE NEXT *AMERICAN NINJA WARRIOR*

Although I have to say that this is a pretty cool goal with amazing side benefits. But let's face facts, your kid probably can't do enough pull-ups to even think about trying.

SHUT UP,
YOUR KID'S NOT THE COOLEST

And if you think your kid is really that cool, you sort of missed the point about what it is to be cool in the first place.

SHUT UP,
YOUR KID'S NOT THE BEST LOOKING

We all love our children, and we all consider them to be the "complete package" of brains and looks. Sorry, it's just not the case. Let it go.

SHUT UP,
YOUR KID'S NOT THE FUNNIEST

Your kid has a great deadpan delivery that is years ahead of their time. Sorry, they are not the next Jerry Seinfeld or Tina Fey.

SHUT UP,
YOUR KID'S NOT THE NEXT JEFF BEZOS

And really, do you want to be some bald dweeb who doesn't take care of his employees, even if it comes with being one of the richest people in the world?

Okay, the side benefits of being Bezos are pretty cool. Being the actual person? Not so much.

SHUT UP,

YOUR KID'S NOT THE NEXT
NATHAN'S HOT DOG EATING CHAMP

Let's face facts: Joey Chestnut is a superhero. If you can eat sixty-three hot dogs in ten minutes while also fighting off a protester in a Darth Vader outfit—which Chestnut actually did in the 2022 contest—you have qualities otherwise not understood by the rest of mankind. You are simply too much for any other human to contemplate. For you parents out there to think that your child could somehow achieve this kind of greatness in competitive eating—which is somehow really a thing—is simply unthinkable.

As well it should be.

SHUT UP,
YOUR KID'S NOT GOING TO BE ON
THE NEW YORK YANKEES

While your son is good at baseball, he's not from the Dominican Republic and hasn't been playing baseball since before he could stand up without falling down, can't hit a slider, and trips over his own two (left) feet. Why not strive for reality and hope he can be a batboy?

SHUT UP,

YOUR KID'S NOT GOING TO GET IN
THE GUINNESS BOOK OF WORLD RECORDS

You know your child's not that great when you pay for them to get in *The Guinness Book of World Records*, and they still can't get in.

SHUT UP,
YOUR KID'S NOT
THE NEXT CALVIN KLEIN MODEL

Driving into the city, seeing that big Calvin Klein billboard, and daydreaming of your child being better-looking than Mark Wahlberg and Kate Moss caused an eight-car pile-up and brought you back to life.

SHUT UP,
YOUR KID'S NOT GOING TO BE
THE NEXT BROADWAY STAR

Just because they've seen every episode of *High School Musical* doesn't mean your theater kid is going to make it on Broadway. Best to let them make it in the high school *Glee* club.

SHUT UP,
YOUR KID'S NOT GOING TO HARVARD

Just because your kid got a 1600 on their SATs, wears glasses, and gets straight As in school doesn't mean they're going to Harvard. In fact, if you're not careful, it's more likely that they'll be a victim of the kid in the car with the bumper sticker, "My son kicked the shit out of your honor student."

SHUT UP,
YOUR KID'S NOT GOING TO
CURE A WORLD DISEASE

So maybe you got your kid some at-home science kits off the internet and your kid also does a great job in his middle school chemistry class. Before you start touting your kid as the next Jonas Salk or Marie Curie, take a chill pill.

Beyond that, understand that chemistry is more collaborative than it's ever been before. With online data sharing and modeling more popular than ever, your kid is more likely to be one of hundreds (if not thousands) of people who contribute to the next great discovery, such as how to cure cancer or eradicate the next great plague.

SHUT UP,
YOUR KID'S NOT GOING TO BE
THE NEXT STEVE JOBS

Actually, the story of Steve Jobs' upbringing is one of the sweetest you can imagine. He was the child of adoptive, working-class parents and a pair of brilliant-yet-oddly-matched biological parents. We'll spare you the details other than to say that Jobs loved his adoptive parents very deeply, his father was a machinist and builder who could intuitively figure out how to build anything from cabinets to a car, and the family just happened to move to Mountain View, California, (the figurative center of Silicon Valley) in 1959 just before the tech boom.

In other words, Jobs is a perfect combination of ability, passion, and opportunity. If you have that combination working for you, you have a really good chance. But just because your kid has thought of a couple of cool apps and loves to take apart computers doesn't mean that he's headed for a career as one of the great computer science engineers of his time and an unparalleled visionary. The closest your kid will get to Steve Jobs is watching a Pixar movie on their iPad.

SHUT UP,

YOUR KID'S NOT GOING TO BE
THE NEXT BOBBY FISCHER

You just got done streaming *Queen's Gambit* for the second time and you're looking at your little girl and thinking, "Aside from abusing drugs and alcohol and dealing with the death of a parent and living in a freaky orphanage and overcoming the dysfunctional life of two weird stepparents, I think she could do that."

And even if your child is one of the boys from *Queen's Gambit*, let it go. By all means, teach your kids how to play chess. It might be the most useful board game in the history of the world in terms of teaching advanced logic and game theory. That said, Fischer's deep-end erratic behavior, which includes disavowing his citizenship and taking a deep dive into anti-Semitism, is hardly worth the risk.

SHUT UP,
YOUR KID'S NOT GOING TO BE AN MMA CHAMPION

J ust because they've watched *The Karate Kid* and *Cobra Kai* doesn't mean they're going to kick ass and take names. Let them work on getting their yellow belt first.

SHUT UP,
YOUR KID'S NOT GOING TO BE
THE NEXT FAMOUS RAPPER

The closest they'll ever get to a recording contract is agreeing to the terms and conditions on Soundcloud.

SHUT UP,
YOUR KID'S NOT GOING TO BE
THE NEXT PENN OR TELLER

In fact, their only magic trick is 52-card Pickup.

SHUT UP,
YOUR KID'S NOT GOING TO BE
THE NEXT HARLEM GLOBETROTTER

For years, the Globetrotters have been doing basketball tricks that defy the laws of physics and logic. They also rarely lose basketball games. Your son's team that just went 3-16 might give him a slight chance of being on the Washington Generals.

SHUT UP,
YOUR KID'S NOT GOING TO BE IN THE CIRCUS

The closest your kid's going to get to an elephant is shoveling elephant shit while working at the Bronx Zoo.

SHUT UP,
YOUR KID'S NOT GOING TO BE
THE NEXT SHAUN WHITE OR TONY HAWK

Just because your kid hits the slopes with the family once a year and can really ace the bunny slope doesn't mean they're ready to compete in the X-Games, and just because they lurk at the local skate park doesn't mean they can do a kickflip or an ollie. Instead of winning a medal, they'll just "win" a series of trips to the ER.

SHUT UP,
YOUR KID'S NOT GOING TO WIN THE NBA DUNK CONTEST

I know your son is six-foot-four, but the only thing he's dunking is donuts.

SHUT UP,
YOUR KID'S NOT THE NEXT DOOGIE HOWSER

S ure, your seven-year-old kid is great at diagnosing illnesses. Whether it's pneumonia, sarcoidosis, or Addison's disease, they really know their illnesses. But before you start envisioning the Dr. before their name, slow down and understand they are really just good at using the WebMD app.

SHUT UP,
YOUR KID'S NOT GOING TO BE A SUPERHERO

J ust because you watched *The Secret World of Alex Mack* growing up, doesn't mean your child is ready to put on a cape and start jumping out of windows to save people's lives. PS—those aren't really windows, they're green screens.

SHUT UP,
YOUR KID'S NOT GOING TO BE ON A STAMP

And if they are on a stamp one day, you're not going to be alive to see it. They probably aren't, either, so just let that one go.

SHUT UP,
YOUR KID'S NOT THE NEXT SUCCESSFUL PODCASTER

Just because you have a microphone and everybody in the world has a podcast doesn't mean your kid is the next Joe Rogan. However, they could wind up being a contestant on *Fear Factor*, where they could eat their own boogers.